It is a cold, winter day in December. A foot of crisp snow lies like a blanket on the ground surrounding a small home in a large oak tree. The tree stands deep in the woods, just outside the big city.

In that cozy home lives, a family of field rats – Mama, Papa and their two children, Woody, and Jessica. Jessica sits for hours by the window watching the pure white snow as it drifts off the windowsill onto the ground, while strong chilly winds blow by. She likes how the snow sparkled on the ground after a big snowfall.

As Jessica watches the snowflakes dancing against a bright sky, her eyes drift to a flower vase on a nearby small table. The vase is frosted, with rose petals centered on the middle of the vase. The vase reminds her about the day that changed her life forever.

This story is about that day – the day Jessica was lost in the big city …

***

It was a few days before Christmas. Jessica sat by the window, as she always did when the snowflakes were tumbling down from the clouds. She stared at the snow, though her thoughts were miles away.

"What will I get Mama and Papa for Christmas?" Jessica wondered.

She had saved all the money she earned by doing odd jobs around the home and the neighborhood. It was not much, because she was only seven years old. But it was just enough to buy a small present.

Jessica sighed. "How am I going to get to the big city? I'm too scared to go on my own," she thought. "And I can't ask Mama, because then my gift won't be a surprise."

Suddenly her eyes settled on Woody, her older brother. He was curled up in the big chair near the log fire, reading a comic.

"Woody, guess what? I have some money saved up," she said.

Woody didn't even look up. "So, why are you telling me?" he replied.

"I want to get a present for Mama and Papa."

"You don't have to do that," said Woody, "I got a present for Mama and Papa. We'll just put your name on it, too."

"No!" Jessica replied firmly.

Woody looked up. "No?" he asked with a frown.

"That's just for babies. I want to get something for them from me by myself. I just want someone to take me to the city tomorrow after school."

Woody read on, ignoring her.

Jessica sighed again. "So, can you?" she asked.

"Can I what?" asked Woody, as he just figured out what she was getting around to asking.

"Take me to the city tomorrow to buy my present …. Please?" she begged.

"All right. I know you are not going to leave me alone. So, I'll take you to the city tomorrow afternoon after school," Woody said, rolling his eyes.

***

The next day after school, Woody met Jessica on the school playground.

"Come on, Jessica. We had better get going. There is not much time for you to look for a present. We must be home before it gets dark. You know Mama does not like us being in that big city alone, especially after dark. It's too dangerous," said Woody, setting off for the city.

Woody talked Mama into going with Jessica. At first, she just shook her head. But then, after thinking it over, she gave in.

"Okay, Woody, you can go. But you give me your word you'll hang on to Jessica. And you must be back home before dark," she said with a serious face.

It was a great day for a walk. There was a gentle, cool breeze and their footsteps crunched in the snow.

After an hour of walking, Woody and Jessica reached the city. They crept through the hole in the wire fence next to the junk store. That was the place all field rats used to enter the city.

As usual, the city was busy. Field rats, like Jessica and Woody, always found the many humans rushing around somewhat overwhelming. Field rats all thought humans were dangerous creatures.

The two little rats dodged the feet of busy Christmas shoppers. Jessica tried her best to keep up with Woody, but it was very difficult. She could feel her throat tightening if he disappeared, even if it was just for a short second.

She stayed off the sidewalk and kept close to the curb, just like all field rats did when they visited the city. When Woody turned the corner for the alley, she barely managed to catch up to him.

"Woody! Don't go so fast! I'm tired. Can't we please sit down for a minute?" she asked, out of breath.

"Okay, but just one minute," Woody replied.

They sat down in a safe spot, looking at the traffic going by. After a short while, Woody got up and took her hand.

"Come, Jessica, we must go. Almost there," he said, encouraging her.

Finally, they reached the underground market that sat under a worn-down building. The door was behind a large dumpster in an alley. Woody and Jessica made their way into the market, which by the looks of it, was in desperate need of some help. The store had very little food and non-food, making it difficult for Jessica to find a nice present for Mama and Papa.

While Jessica looked for a gift, she overheard two rats speaking. It was the store manager, Chester, talking to one of his regular customers.

"Hay, Chester, what happened? Did they get you again?" asked the customer.

"Yes, last night by those Hoods," answered Chester. "It was the third time this month! I'm telling you; those gangster sewer rats are going to put me out of business. I am going broke replacing what they took. It's getting harder to live in this part of the city."

Jessica's heart started to beat faster. This scared her very much. "Mama is right. The city is a dangerous place. I don't want to stay in this place any longer than I must, she thought.

At last, Jessica found a gift for Mama and Papa. It was a beautiful, frosted vase, with dainty rose pedals painted on it. She went to Chester, who stood behind the till.

"Well, well, young lady, what can I do for you?" Chester said as he beamed at the little field rat.

Jessica proudly took her money out of her pocket. "I'm buying a Christmas present for my Mama and Papa," she said, smiling broadly.

"Oh, they are going to like your present very much. Let me wrap the vase in bubble wrap so it won't break."

Chester handed her the wrapped vase and she put it into her rucksack to take it home.

"Be careful, and hurry home," Chester called as she and Woody took off for home.

It was starting to get dark, and it was a long walk home. It was hard getting through the streets this time; the streets seem to be busier than before.

This time, it seemed Woody was going even faster. Jessica tried her best to keep up with him, but all she could see was his shadow, as he skillfully dodged the speeding cars.

Suddenly, she was knocked off her feet by a shower of freezing water, caused by a truck driving through a puddle of water. Jessica gasped as the water washed her into a dark, empty hole. Sputtering, she got to her feet. She looked around but couldn't see much of the little light that entered the hole from above. A horrible, raw stench hit her little nose.

"Oh, no! I've landed in the sewer!" Jessica cried.

To Jessica's horror, she saw that the water at her feet was starting to rise.

"Woody! Woody! Help me, please!" she shouted, tears starting to run down her furry little cheeks.

Suddenly, a wave of stinking water swept her down the sewer tunnel. Jessica thrashed about desperately, trying hard to find something to cling to. Luckily, a rusty nail snagged her rucksack. She grabbed the edge of the tunnel, and with her last strength, she managed to pull herself through the rusted metal bars that covered the sewer drain hole.

"Where am I?" she cried.

She found herself on the city streets again, but nothing looked familiar to her. She was in another part of town – a part she didn't know at all.

"Woody! Woody! Woody!" screamed Jessica, panicking.

It did no good; Woody was nowhere to be found. The thing she had feared most had happened. Jessica was lost in the big city. Tears rolled down her sad little face as she watched human figures passing by. She was all alone.

"Now what am I going to do? Christmas is two days away, and I'm stuck here in the city alone," cried Jessica.

Scared and cold, she had to get away from the busy humans. She crept into a space behind a dumpster in a nearby alley and cried herself to sleep.

***

Early the next morning, Jessica woke up to a cold, dark, empty street. The only things moving were the snowplows, clearing the streets for another busy morning. It looked as though several inches of snow had fallen since Jessica went to sleep.

"Where am I?" Jessica wondered.

Then, the awful reality hit her. She was lost in the big city. By this time, she was very hungry. Jessica's whiskers twitched. What was that lovely smell? It was food!

She took off to find the source of the smell. Her nose led her to an alley behind the mall. Large trash cans were lined against the wall of a building.

There, just a few feet away, was a large piece of meat just waiting for her to eat. Jessica ran as fast as she could. She stretched out her little paws to pick up the meat and closed her eyes to take that first bite.

Suddenly, she was knocked to the ground by a large sewer rat. He grabbed the meat and scurried away into a nearby building. Jessica, being a field rat, lived in a house where she used to eat food out of a garden. She didn't know what it was like to have to search for food.

Jessica started looking for anything to nibble on around the garbage cans. She thought about her family, Mama and Papa waiting for their little girl to come home; so that they could be together. That was what she wanted the most. Being lost in the big city was the last thing she ever expected or wanted. At that moment, she wanted to be as far away from the city as possible, sitting at home safe and sound.

Jessica was so busy thinking about her family and looking for a bite to eat that she never noticed the large black cat that was sitting on top of a dumpster.

"Mmm, what do we have here?" purred the feline as it sat on the dumpster, cleaning himself.

Unfortunately for Jessica, she was about to learn rule number one of surviving in the city – always be aware of what goes on around you. As she continued her hunt for food, blissfully unaware of the danger, the sleek black cat set himself up to pounce.

"Mmmm, the little rat is much smaller than the other rats here in the city. It must be a field rat who obviously knows nothing about surviving in the big city. This catch should be easy," purred the black cat, licking his whiskers with delight, as he plotted his next move.

The black cat jumped down from the dumpster, and stealthily crept up to Jessica. She was sitting on the ground, whiskers twitching, as she was sniffing the air for another source of food.

As she turned around to go toward another dumpster, the cat pounced. Jessica squealed with fright and did the first thing she could do; run for her life. She scampered to the nearest hole she could see.

The cat hissed angrily as Jessica disappeared into the hole. She sat down, struggling to get her breath.

"Goodbye, black cat. I'm safe," she gasped.

When she turned around to see where she was, a shiver ran down her spine. Eight large black sewer rats surrounded Jessica.

"Oh, no! It's the rat gang the shopkeeper spoke about! It's the Hoods!" she thought desperately.

"What do we have here?" asks a rat with a cap, who goes by the name of Rico.

They looked at her with large, yellow eyes. "What are we going to do with her?" asked one of the other Hoods, a large rat with a patch covering his left eye. He is called Von.

Another member, Mourice spoke up, "I'm sure we can find something for her to do."

"She's a country rat," said Rico, moving in closer for a better look. "Maybe she can cook and clean for us. I've heard country rats are good cooks."

"Who are you? Where did you come from?" asked the largest of the rats. He wore a gold chain around his neck and goes by the name Odis.

Jessica quivered with fear and backed into a corner before answering, "My name is Jessica, I'm from Spring Lake. I … I … I came here with my brother to buy a gift for Mama and

Papa, but I got lost here. I didn't know this was your nest. I was running from a big black cat …

I'll leave now."

"Leave?" said Odis, as he winked at the other rats. "Who said anything about leaving? You don't need to go. Stick around; the party is just beginning."

Von noticed the bag Jessica was carrying. "Hey, let's see what's in the bag. Maybe she bought something for the party," he said.

He lunged at Jessica and grabbed the bag from her.

"Hey! Give that back!" demanded Jessica.

Rico looked through her bag, and they found the vase that she had bought her parents for Christmas.

Rico held the vase in the air. "What is this?" he asked.

"Here! Let me see?" requested Mourice.

Rico threw it to him.

"It looks like some kind of vase," said Mourice before throwing it to another member.

As they tossed the vase back and forth, Jessica watched in horror. The gift she had bought with the only money she had almost fell to the floor, before she grabbed it.

"Stop! Stop this now!"

The rats stopped in their tracks, stunned into silence by a voice from behind. Everyone, including Jessica turned around. It was an old, grey rat, the oldest member of the pack.

Odis spoke up, "Sire, we were just talking about what we are going to do with our young visitor here."

"She will stay here with us," said the wise old rat.

"What are you doing Master Cyrus? She is a field rat; she doesn't belong here," said Von.

"She is from the country, that is true. But she is also a rodent like us, and she needs our protection from the dangers out there. She does not know how to survive in our world," explained Cyrus.

Jessica sighed with relief. She was grateful for the offer; she felt a sense of comfort knowing that she would be safe from the many dangers that were lurking outside.

***

Hours went by as Jessica ran through the city streets, with her new friends. As they wandered through the kitchens of houses and restaurants, Jessica discovered much about surviving in the city. There was never enough food. The food they found came from trash bins. Jessica was not used to this since she was born and raised in the country. She was used to eating fresh meat from the hunt of the week, along with fresh nuts, berries, and food from the garden. And she quickly learned that she had to have a cold heart. A rat that cared about others was a dead rat.

***

Meanwhile, back in the deep woods, Woody finally got home. He dreaded telling Mama and Papa that he lost Jessica in the big city while Christmas shopping. Woody knew that Mama and Papa were not going to take it well, especially the way Mama felt about that city. There was a storm coming, and it would be impossible to find her with all the dangers in the dark.

As Woody suspected, Mama was upset.

"Don't worry, dear," Papa comforted Mama. "I will bring Jessica home, even if it takes me all day and night to find her. Come on, Woody, show me where you were when Jessica disappeared."

***

It's been an hour since Papa, Woody, and the other field rats, who offered to help in the search, took off for the city. Mama was getting worried that they would be lost in the storm. She watched the snowflakes coming down hard, covering tracks that were left by Papa and Woody. She knew there was nothing she could do except to wait patiently.

By the time Papa, Woody, and the rest of the country rats reached the city, there was a foot of snow and more falling. It was getting tougher to walk and they couldn't see very well in the blowing snow. They knew it was not going to be easy to look for Jessica in the storm, in the dark, and they were right.

***

Back at the Hoods' nest, they were preparing for the coming storm. Cyrus sent a few of the younger rats to find food for storage before the storm, while others stayed behind to prepare the nest.

Cyrus was busy thinking about their newest member to the colony. His plan to convert her into a city rat was working. He kept her close to the pack and took the food she found. However, he had to remember she was still a field rat. And then there was her family to consider. He knew that they would be looking for her.

"I must think of other ways to keep her in the colony," Cyrus thought.

***

Jessica had spent hours working with a few rats collecting food for storage. Snow continued falling, and the bitter chill of the winds rushed through her thick, snow-white fur. She knew she had to find some shelter from the storm and soon.

"Hey, Jess, I know an old, abandoned building we can go to. Humans use it when they need shelter from the cold winds. I hide in there all the time. We could warm up in there," said Odis. He was one of the younger Hoods, and Jessica liked him. He wasn't nasty like some of the others.

Jessica's heart was thumping in her chest. She was always told that humans mean trouble and here were many of them!

Odis and the others did not seem to show fear. In fact, they were taking food off the plates of these humans. One took a piece of bread right from a woman's hand. When she tried to swat him; he bit her and took off.

From what she saw, these humans could barely stand on their own two feet. They had very little strength to fight off the predators that were taking their food. They only had the clothes on their backs and a few heavy blankets to keep them warm from the heavy storm that raged outside.

Jessica saw that these humans were easy to get around, and she knew she would need to hunt for her food if she wanted to eat. So, without hesitation, she went over to a plate of food, grabbed a large piece of meat, and ran off with it.

Suddenly, a little girl cried out.

Jessica stopped in her tracks. She turned around and saw a little dark-haired girl about the age of two, pointing to her.

The cry brought out the compassion for life she had almost forgotten she had. Remorse flooded her heart. Jessica ran to the little girl, placed the piece of meat back on her plate, took off to find her friends waiting outside.

Odis was furious. "Where have you been, and where is your food?" he snarled.

She hesitated before she replied, "I lost it while running."

Jessica didn't dare tell him the real reason for losing the food. They would simply not understand that she gave it up to a hungry child. This was the first time Jessica had seen Odis act this way.

"Well, what are you waiting for?" chided Odis. "Go back and get another piece, or else you'll be out on the street."

Jessica had no choice but to go back and get another piece of food. Fortunately, someone had left some food on their plate before going off to sleep. It wasn't much, but it was enough to feed a couple rats. So, she inched toward the plate and grabbed the piece of ham.

Suddenly, a large hand came down, nearly crushing her. She saw the shadow just in time to move out of the way. Jessica took off as quickly as her little legs could carry her.

***

Woody was scurrying through the alleys, looking for Jessica. As he turned the corner, he saw a small rat with white fur running with a pack of black and brown rats. Although the blowing snow made it difficult to see clearly, Woody knew there was only one that had pure white fur like that; she was the only one of their kind.

She must have made friends with the city rats to find shelter and food," Woody thought. He turned around and ran back to Papa and the others to tell them that he had found Jessica.

"Papa! Papa! I've found Jessica!" Woody shouted when he saw Papa and the others in the next alley.

Out of breath, he told him about the other rats. Papa's face turned hard.

"There is only one colony that rules this side of the city – the Hoods. That means she is with my old nemesis, Cyrus," he gravely told the other country rats.

"Cyrus? Who is Cyrus?" asked Uncle Gary, who lived next-door to Mama and Papa.

Papa sighed. "Before we moved to the country, my wife and I lived in the city. At that time, I ran with the city rats."

The other country rats gasped.

"We needed a place to live. So, Cyrus, a friend of mine at the time, invited us to stay and live with his colony. But things changed. Food that I had gone to find for my wife, and I was eaten up by the other rats. The living conditions were terrible. It was cold, dirty, and crowded. There were many things I hated about living in the city, but the one thing I hated the most were the many dangers we had to face every day in the streets. There were other sewer rats from another part of town, the stray cats that hang out in the alleys, and of course there were humans, our worst enemy. It was not the type of environment I wanted to raise my family. So, when my wife and I discovered we were expecting a family soon, we moved to the country."

The other rats listened to his story in awe, not one even twitched a whisker.

"We knew it was not going to be easy, being that we were from the city, the only life we knew. We knew we would have to build our own home, hunt, and kill for our food, where in the city we only had to look for scraps of food. But we knew we would not be crowded or have to worry about other rats taking our food, and our environment would be safe. It was the right thing to do, but I knew it would not be easy leaving the big city without a showdown with Cyrus. He felt I had turned my back on him and the colony."

"Have you ever seen Cyrus after that time?" asked Woody.

Papa sighed. "No, I had no reason to ever visit. Cyrus made it very clear that he never wanted to see me again. I had hoped that with time, Cyrus would get over his resentment. But now he has Jessica, which means that we will meet again. Now we must hurry to find her!"

***

Meanwhile, on the other side of the street, Jessica, Odis, and the others had gone into a large kitchen of a restaurant. Nobody was there, so the rats went to work hunting down food in the storage bins. The sewer rats knew about the traps the humans set out to rid them of pests and where they were set, so they knew how to work around them without getting caught.

While they grabbed all the food they could get, a light came on and then they heard footsteps that were heading toward the big kitchen. All the rats took off for the door. One of them had forgotten about the traps and was caught. As Jessica ran to the door, she heard a loud,

"Squeak!!"

She went back in to see who it was, the light was still on, but no one was in sight. Jessica tried to make her way to the other side of the room before anyone came in. When the human came back, Jessica hid behind some boxes that stood against the wall. After the large male human figure left, she went to find out who was caught in the trap.

When she reached the trap, she gasped. It was Tony, one of Odis's friends. It was too late. The trap was a smoke bomb used to destroy pests at first contact. Tears welled up in her eyes. It was going to be very difficult to tell Odis.

Jessica left the kitchen to meet the others outside. Her heart felt heavy. For the first time since she started running with the pack, she realized how much danger there really was on the streets. The dangers Mama warned her about, especially for her kind.

But Jessica shook off the bad feeling. This was her home now. She went to look for her friends. As Jessica walked out the kitchen door, she walked into a foot of snow. The storm had let up to light drifts that laid like a light blanket on the snow that had fallen hard just hours before. The fresh snow glistens when the moonlight hits it just right. As Jessica took a turn for the right, she heard a familiar voice from behind.

"Jessica! Jessica!"

She turned around. It was Papa and Woody. Suddenly, Jessica ran in the opposite direction. She was not ready to return home, because she had learned to adapt to the life of the city.

"Jessica! Jessica! Where are you going?" cried Papa, surprised to see she did not come to him.

"Papa why is she running away from us?" asked Woody.

"I'm afraid my worst fear has happened. She has become one of them," replied Papa, saddened at the recognition. "Let's follow her."

Papa, Woody, and the others tried to follow her through the streets. As they ran down through the side streets, they found themselves in another dark alley; the same alley Jessica found herself in when she met the pack.

***

Jessica and the other rats arrived back at the nest. Out of breath, they told Cyrus that Jessica's family were on their trail and heading their way.

Cyrus smiled, but the smile didn't reach his eyes. "Oh, I would love to see my old friend again. All of you, go out to welcome them!"

While Papa and the others turned the corner to the alley, they were greeted by the pack. They then noticed that they were surrounded. This pack Papa had recognized as the pack he used to run with.

Just then Papa had heard a familiar voice from behind him.

"Hello, old friend. It has been a long time."

Papa turned around. Standing there before him, was his old friend, Cyrus.

"Cyrus, so we meet again. I see you are the same as I remember," Papa said, sighing.

"You still manage control over the colony, now you are recruiting field rats. What's the matter, not enough rats to work for you?"

"You turned your back on us when you left years ago. Someone had to take control. If it were not for me, these rats would not have survived here in this city," snarled Cyrus.

"I left the city, not my fellow rats. It was not a place I wanted to raise my family. I am happy where I am. It's a place where I know my family will be safe. City life is not for me. Nobody should have to live like this," explained Papa, as he waved his arm to the side in a gesture to the city streets and alleys.

"Not even a rat," he added as he turned his attention to his daughter. "Come Jessica, let's go home."

"No, I am staying here with my friends." snapped Jessica, defying her father's wishes.

"What?" replied Papa. "This is not a game … I said let's go … Now!"

"I'm not going," Jessica repeated, as she stood in defiance, among her friends.

"We here like the city life. We can handle it. We are Hood rats. Rats who live in the country become weak. That is what happened to you, you have become soft. Your own daughter doesn't even want to go home with you," sneered Cyrus.

Papa was getting angry. He knew he couldn't fight like he once did. He was outnumbered by eight rats, and besides, he had his children there. He was not the same rat that used to run the streets a long time ago. He had to realize after peering into the eyes of his children Woody and Jessica, seeing the concern on his son's face and the careless look on Jessica's face, who was obviously a part of the city now; his family came first. He knew he had to find some way to get his daughter away from Cyrus' influence. The only way Papa was going to get out of this, was to convince them to change their way of life. By the looks of things, this was not going to be easy. But it was the only way he was going to save his daughter.

"Is this how you want to spend the rest of your lives? Living in crowded nests, with very little food to go around, risking your lives on these streets and alleys?" Papa asked.

Von answered, "We can handle living in the city. We are survivors."

"We have to stay together," said Rico. "It's the only way we are going to stay alive here in the city."

"That is what I am trying to tell you. You don't have to worry about surviving in the big city. You can live in the country in peace, without the control of others," Papa protested. He was thinking about the control he was once under when he ran through the streets with his friend Cyrus, before he turned on him.

Mourice spoke up, "All colonies need a leader, to help stay together, to watch our backs."

Papa just shook his head in disappointment. "I can't believe you are willing to give up your freedom this easy," he said.

"It may have been what you wanted, to leave the colony and the city to find a safer place to live; but this right here, is what we want, we are making it just fine," answered Odis.

"You say you are making it. This is what Cyrus here wants you to believe. I have a story about surviving I would like to tell you. It happened a few years ago, while I was still with the colony. Then food was in very short supply in our area at the time, we had to have food, as it was falling on winter soon. I had wandered away from the nest to look for more. As I got further away from the nest, I found myself on the major highway trying to avoid getting hit by passing cars, while trying to find a safe path. I had worked my way down the main highway. I found myself in a large yard, facing a large white building."

Papa paused before he proceeded. It seemed as if he was thinking about something very unpleasant.

"I wandered into the building and made my way down a large passage without being seen. Down another passageway, into a small white room … There, I saw a plate of food and ran for it, that was until I heard voices. I turned toward the door, and there I saw a tall white male human, put into the room with me. I tried running for the door when it shut in my face. There I was, in a room with four white walls and a hungry human for company. I had only the crumbs from the human's plate to satisfy my hunger and some liquid from a metal cup to quench my thirst. Most of the time I had to keep myself from getting caught by the human, who at the time would be willing to get rid of me anyway he can just for something to do.

"Finally, the door to his room opened for the human. While it was open, I took the opportunity and ran out as quickly as I could. That was the closest I ever want to get to death. It's true, you need to stick together, but we also need to build more than just strength with each other for protection. We need to build trust as well. You need to fight for peace. You do have freedom to choose," explained Papa.

A sudden warm feeling of peace came over him. As he looked over at Jessica, he noticed a look of concern on her face. "I hope I've reached you, my child." Papa thought.

"That is enough!" shouted Cyrus, growing impatient. "You are wasting my time and making excuses to avoid the truth. You are a coward for running away."

"I speak the truth, and you know it. You have these rats so convinced that this life is the only thing there is, they don't even realize they do have freedom to choose. You took that away from them," replied Papa. He was angry and determined to take away the control Cyrus had over these confused rodents, especially his daughter, who was starting to come around.

Cyrus was getting even more impatient. He knew Papa was speaking the truth, and he knew that he didn't have long before he had to step down as leader over the colony. He didn't want his colony to know the truth. If they did, he would lose his control over the pack and lose his position as leader. So, Cyrus did the only thing he could, to gain some control over the colony while he still held the position as their leader.

"Attack!" shouted Cyrus in sheer anger. Nobody moved.

Odis stood in the shadow. He was to be Cyrus' replacement one day. He had been listening to what Papa had to say. It got him to think about making some changes when he does take over the nest, and by the looks of things it is going to be sooner than he thinks.

"I gave you an order … Attack!" Cyrus demanded.

As the Hood rats started to make their move toward Papa and the others, Odis shouted, "Wait!"

He looked at Jessica. Although Jessica had spent some time running the streets with the city rats, Odis saw that she also had her freedom. Something he never had. Now that he will become the next leader, it's time for some changes.

He smiled at Jessica and said, "Go, you don't belong here, your family needs you."

Odis then turned around to face Cyrus. "And as for you Cyrus, I'm no longer taking orders from you."

"You defy me. Do you know who I am?" shouted Cyrus, who was not only surprised but angry at the way his colony was acting. "What is going on here, Odis? Are you going to listen to a field rat that turned his back on us? Are you turning soft on me, too? You are not the leader yet. While I am the leader, you will listen to me and follow my orders. Is that clear?"

"No!" cried Odis. He had enough with the treatment he was getting from Cyrus for the past few years and wanted to put an end to it once and for all. "We are through serving you, Cyrus. As of now you no longer hold the position as our leader. I am taking over and there will be changes. From this day forward, you rats will have your own freedom to choose."

He looked at the Hoods. Odis knew it was not going to be easy for his fellow rats to adjust. But with help from some friends, as he looked over at Papa and Jessica, he could make it. There is one thing Odis overlooked though: the traditional fight for leadership.

"Not so fast, you forget that you must earn the right to that position – a fight to the death. Believe me, I will show no mercy. I will win," warned Cyrus with a look of determination on his old, worn face.

Odis thought about how intense this fight would be, and how much it would mean for him to win. He also realized that Cyrus was one of the toughest fighters in that part of the city, which meant that his life would be on the line. He and Cyrus prepared themselves for the fight of their lives, as they circled each other, surrounded by the Hoods.

Suddenly, Cyrus made the first move. He jumped on Odis, trying to grab his neck. He ended up getting Odis's back. Cyrus grabbed hold of Odis's skin with his razor-sharp teeth. Odis tried hard to shack him off but knew the only way to release the grip would be to bite him back. He and Odis fought for a while, until Odis took Cyrus by surprise and jumped on him with his razor-sharp teeth. Odis knew it would not be long now before he would become the new leader.

"Odis … STOP! You don't have to do this," cried Jessica.

Odis heard her, but ignored it, as he was close to winning, and Cyrus was close to defeat. But then, something happened to Odis. First, he saw the snow falling. Then, he heard Christmas songs sung by people walking on the main streets. Odis felt something deep within himself, a feeling of warmth and compassion perhaps, something he never felt for anyone before. He let go of the grip he had on Cyrus and got off him.

"What are you doing?" asked Cyrus, who was on the ground in a heap, defeated. He added, "Finish the job. I do not wish to live like this."

"No, it's not worth it. Go on, crawl back to your hole and bother us no more," Odis said, still panting from the fight.

As the colony of rats rejoiced, Cyrus crawled off into the sewers in defeat. Jessica then noticed something in the sky.

"Papa, Papa look!" she shouted, trying to get everyone to listen.

When she did get their attention, she pointed to the sky. When they looked up, they saw a bright star lighting up the whole sky, finally clear after the long storm. A blissful feeling came over all of them, especially the Hood rats. It appears that there was a miracle on Christmas Eve after all.

Papa looked up. "It's the North Star. It truly is Christmas. We made it," he said.

"Not yet," replied Woody. "We still have to make it home, before Christmas morning."

"You are right, let's go," sighed Papa.

"Thank you," said Odis to Papa, Woody, and especially Jessica, for opening his eyes to the truth.

"Why don't you live in the country with us?" asks Jessica.

Odis thought that over for a moment, then answered with a deep sigh, "Nah. It's a tempting offer, but I better stay here. These guys need me. I'll come and visit some time."

Odis then took off through the alley to catch up with the others, as Papa, his family, and the other field rats headed for home.

While they were walking along, Jessica spoke up. "Papa, I'm sorry I left and got lost in the city. I just wanted to get you and Mama a Christmas present. I really wanted to get you something special," she said sadly. "But I left it at the nest, I'll go get it. Wait for me."

She quickly ran back to the nest, grabbed her bag, and then ran back to Papa and the others.

"I have the present, I'm ready to go," said Jessica, smiling broadly.

"Ha, ha, ha, that's okay. You know, just finding you and having all of us together for Christmas would have been our present," laughed Papa, as he hugged both Jessica and Woody. "Let's hurry home now that it is clear. We can make it before daylight. The storm had let up, and it is Christmas Day."

***

Later on, Christmas Day, Jessica gave her present to Mama and Papa. They loved the frosted vase they received. But that didn't matter. She had an experience that changed her life. She had seen a world she never knew existed. Going back with Papa and Woody to her safe world, in the country with her family for Christmas, was all that mattered to her … She was finally home.

***

Sitting by her window, as she returns to the present, Jessica shudders as she thinks about her experience of being homeless and lost. Through the hardships that both rats and humans must endure, they still manage to hold on to the belief and the spirit of Christmas, giving some hope to stay together with their loved ones, and others to just keep going, so that they can see beyond tomorrow. If we believe in miracles, there will always be Christmas.

The End

www.ingramcontent.com/pod-product-compliance
Lightning Source LLC
Chambersburg PA
CBHW041822110726
48006CB00019B/2482